SEASON

BY RITU AHLAWAT

INDIA • SINGAPORE • MALAYSIA

ISBN
Paperback 979-8-89610-372-1
Hardcase 979-8-89699-434-3

Telling someone how you feel

is like bringing a blind person into your heart,

introducing them to everything you have inside,

by holding and guiding their hands.

The first person that comes to visit you

gets you very excited,

and you try to show every tiny detail of your heart's room.

First, you're shy,

then you insist;

in the end, you cry.

Now you've locked your heart—

nobody's gonna come and dirty my house.

Heavy rain, thunder—

someone is knocking for help.

"Open, open it!"

But all you care about is the dirt in your house.

Contents

Foreword

Life is a mix of seasons—some messy, some beautiful, and some that don't make sense until much later. This book isn't about the seasons outside, but the ones that unfold within us—the silent storms, the moments of growth, the warmth of love, and the cold of loss.

Season holds pieces of me, written over years when words were my only escape. These poems don't explain themselves; they just are—like me, constantly evolving. If you're looking for something perfect or polished, this isn't it. But if you're open to raw moments, real emotions, and truth with a bit of sarcasm here and there, then welcome. Maybe you'll find something here that feels like your own season too.

Ritu

Spring

Poem of Love

If there were a poem, dear,

That could narrate my love,

That could spill my heart out,

Then I would have offered you that.

As I read the Shakespeare,

Turned pages of Oscar Wilde,

But baby, neither am I Juliet,

Nor the Queen of Chess.

The worldly words are so scant,

And honey, our story is so divergent.

So I poured the ink on a blank space,

And my heart offered words a direction.

I closed my eyes and found your face,

Instantly, it was perfect with your gaze.

Here I am, giving you this Poem of Love,

As 'I love you' is never enough.

I hope you remember these words,

When you're lonely or feeling unsure.

No matter what life puts you through,

Or what may try to hold you back,

Remember always, you're never alone,

Remember always; you can never be torn.

You are not one from the crowd,

You will surely not die unknown.

My words will always keep you alive,

My words will always be your part,

My words will leave a permanent mark—

As, darling,

You are loved with my whole heart.

Lucky Ones

What would it be like to
write something lasting,
so beautiful that age
won't define.

Something
like a
fine wine
gets better with time

Lucky are the souls who leave,
Yet keep their words in ink,
They come alive
Each time
You read their lines.

The Boy

He was The Boy,

She was just the other girl.

He was The World,

And she was just another thing in it.

Love, only a game for him,

But look, she was in love with him.

His head always held high,

She couldn't bear the look in his eyes.

The moon, oh, shinier than before,

A smile, no, didn't need any reason to soar.

Music in every sound she hears,

As if the winds were singing her song.

But the truth had to be revealed,

No more moments for lies.

The show had begun—

Call it Showtime,

The mask pulled off, her feet left the ground.

A hurricane in her soul,

"No, this can't be the truth,"

She lost control.

Betrayed in love for all she had done,

"Why me?

Among billions in the whole wide world?"

Either accept it or lose to the lie—

The work is done, no turning around.

It's been a long time now;

She's still the other girl.

The world is now just the world to her.

The winds are whispering something to her—

"Listen carefully.

Is this her song?"

Messy hair, No makeup

Messy hair and no makeup on,
An old t-shirt with a bright smile worn—
That's what she wore
The other day on a date with him.

Profound conversations and great food,
They drove back home, all pleased.

"Oh, I wish I could've made an effort to look good,"
She advised herself
In her thoughtful mind.

Something he said

Brought her back to the real-time

"You're the most beautiful face

I've seen in all my life."

He kissed her lips,

They slept holding each other tight.

What a lucky girl,

Don't you think she is?

Being loved for

Who she is every night.

Infinite

My love for you cannot be said in one line;

It is more like a color filling my life.

I love you like the sky loves the color blue,

Or the land loves the color green.

My love for you is as pure,

My love for you is as true.

My love for you cannot be said in one poem;

My love for you demands a paper the size of infinite.

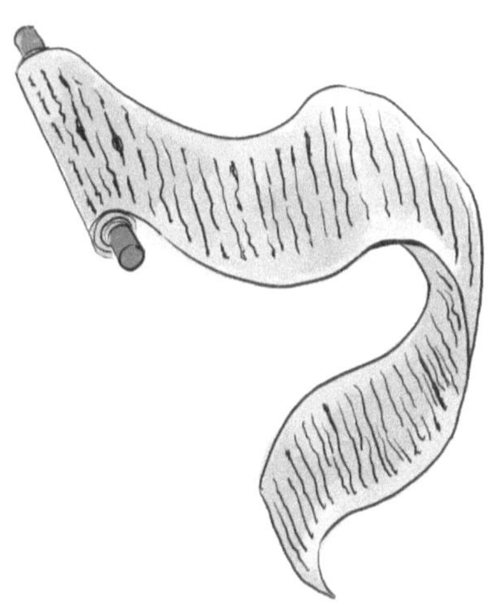

Dreams come true

Yesterday was beautiful,

Today will be better.

Nothing stays the same.

Life happens every second.

There's eternity to explore;

You haven't seen a lot.

Fireflies in a dark forest,

Bonfire in the cold,

Soft music and wild sounds—

The universe talks amid the crowds.

Night whispers,

The moon is alive,

Trees interact,

Insects organize.

The sun always shines bright,

No matter how dark the previous night.

Dreams will come true,

If you dare to write.

F.R.I.E.N.D

From the heavens above,

Below the blue skies at crossroads,

I found a friend to get along,

And now, I am never traveling alone.

I was gifted red from all colors,

My blues he stole away.

From the collection of my coal,

He turned diamonds all his way.

He is so in love,

And so am I.

He'll be there at my sunsets,

And I'll be there at his sunrise.

That's how I believe we'll live,

And I hope we circle back one day.

Stimulation

Constant brain stimulation,

Stuck up in our minds,

Flexible yet stubborn,

We're curious all the time.

Unfiltered beliefs,

Giving up on prejudice.

The soul is a mirror,

Peeking from all sides.

A Time-Traveller

A time-traveler,
That's what he is.
Every word from his lips—
No boundaries they seek.

His dreams are broken,
Cracks cover the picture.
Put a bucket on the surface—
Who's got the time to fix it?

21st-century old-fashioned,
Modernized in an ancient school.
Spiritual, yet a drunk...
Restless and intense.
Loyal, yet a rebel,
Lazy, with an active thought.

Stuck between two universes—

The one he lives in,

The other he desires.

And when he sings,

Here comes the spring again :)

An untouched voice touches the soul.

A baby sparrow gets food from its mom.

Careless.

What an emotional fool!

He cries in a veil;

His love bursts like a splash.

This boy is no different.

This boy is unique.

This boy seems to have nothing.

Yet, this boy has it all.

The Poetry of You

Words keep coming to me.

Poems are swimming in wild waters,

waves are dancing in your oceans.

Tucked away for so long,

silenced.

Why?

Because I'm thinking about you.

And I will remember

And I will remember
The way you smell
The music of your breath

And I will remember
The wink in your eye
Your pink cheeks when you smile

And I will remember
The way you kissed
No time did you waste
Your lips on my neck
One of my greatest highs

And I will remember
The innocence in your eyes
Your childlike smile
An ocean in your gaze
My mind sinking inside

And I will remember
When our fingers touched
The racing of my heart
When you held me so close
The world clock stopped

Summer

Breathe the New Winds

As the night casts its gloom,

Darkness becomes clearer—

It's a prison of fallen stars.

My new home,

Where I belong—

Bitter and sweet,

The taste of lost memories.

Now free and alive,

I can breathe the new winds.

Only a seed back then,

Now my branches kiss the sky.

It is the start of a new life,

Beneath a sheet of new sky.

More than love

Why lust for words,
While silence can recite it all perfect?
Every flash beside you—
A sign of fantasy springing to life.

I won't say the stars are more silver,
Or that the sky is more blue.
Everything's alike as it was—
Nothing has reversed so far.

Since that's the beauty of your charm—
Making all things worthy as they are.

This time I'll pretend to be blind
So I can see the universe with your eyes.
The deeper I go there,
The more divine view I find.

I am not sure what it is
That rushes into my blood,
But this is "Something More Than Love."
Believe me!
Because I've been in love before.

Perfect Woman?

Destroying yourself feels so good sometimes.

A little bit of smoke,

Too much alcohol.

I'm no perfect woman,

Never aimed for it,

Never can be.

But what is a perfect woman?

Who controls herself?

Compromises?

Sacrifices?

Lives for everyone—

But herself?

I destroy myself,

A little bit of smoke,

Too much alcohol.

Self-Obsessed

No. You cannot be sad.
How dare you?
You are beautiful. You've got a job.
You live in a big city. You have a home.

What are your worries made up of?
What are you thinking?
Superficial thoughts must be.

Don't tell me that
you feel insecure,
hopeless, and bored;
that existential questions occupy your head,
and your consciousness is mostly vague;
that you've read brilliant minds
but cannot apply it in your own life.

I forbid you to take that road.

Your problems are smaller than a grain.

My condolences to your chronic brain.

What a self-obsessed, bloody human!

Finding darkness in the solace of a demon,

declaring light an illusion.

You are arguing that winter is the only season.

Better sleep than using your sight.

Your eyes will be rejected by the blind.

Responsible

I can never write like Bukowski;
Oh, I really wish I could.

But for that,
I need a crappy life:
Many fucked-up whores,
Addiction to alcohol,
Ten packs of cigarettes a day,
Always short on cash,
And a not-so-kind landlord.

It is the second of July today;
I paid my rent—yesterday.

Where?

Where are the readers?
The ones who feel.

Where are the listeners?
The ones who perceive.

Where are the speakers?
The ones who believe.

Where are the lovers?
The ones who worship.

Where are the broken?
The ones who dream.

Where are the crazy?
The ones who live?

One Rule

When you feel like getting low,

And they can sense it in your hello,

Don't open up your heart at once,

As the blues come easy,

And the blues go tough.

You craft a smile so bright, my love,

That your lows turn into the glow you deserve.

I know it's easier said than done,

Or they'll crush your soul on the count of ten.

There is just one rule in the making:

It's your life; you have to own it.

Read it until you believe it.

Baby, fake it until you make it.

Finding My Way

My quest on a forsaken road,
Approaching a peculiar abode.
Palms striving second hand to hold—
I confess I miss my beloved!

Time, one fine day, will change.
Hard work, that day, will bestow a reward.
In the meanwhile, dear God,
Let me look up to the sky,
Never down on another life.

The good books that I read
Say that bad loses in the end.
In my quest on a forsaken road,
I embrace good to conquer the wrong.

Lost Passion

Do you know
what I liked about you?

How passionate you were—
about your work,
about your life.

You saw beauty in everything.

But you started losing that.
In fact, we both did.

You weren't the only one;
devils spoke to me some nights, too.

A luxury

Experience
Goes never out of fashion,
Experience
Remains always on trend.

Speak the truth,
Ask that girl,
Travel the unknown road,
Kiss a stranger,
Let love explode.
Experience
It is for everybody,
A luxury
In the simplest of tasks

Everything Everywhere All at Once

Even though I've broken your heart,
we both still exist in this life.

I don't need to do laundry and taxes with you—
your presence alone is enough.

By the way, I watched that movie for the third time;

it becomes more captivating every time.

Confessions of a
Wannabe Poet

I am a lousy writer
who loves to write,
one of a kind.
Shakespeare would've vomited
had he lived in my time.

I think I'm so deep,
unfolding mysteries of this age—
when in reality, just an idiot,
scattering blindly, page by page.

Rain

Rain

Rain, oh rain...

Are you what I only want?

From the sky, from the eyes...

Pour my heart; do the rebirth.

Make me new; heal what hurts!

Heaven should drown in the flood of hopes.

Hell should receive the snow at the top.

I lost my love when I felt the most,

Burned down desires with the fire that was fake!

Now I am slowly waking up,

Up with some true belief.

I'll take a step,

The step towards myself.

Where can I find what I've lost.

Love, even if it hurts...

Where I can ride in the snow

And swim in the flood!

Oh! dear God,

Where are you hiding?

Some say in locked doors,

Some state in open hearts...

Ignoring all the thoughts,

There's a voice I can hear.

I am here; I am here.

Look this way, my child!

Don't look too close,

Don't go that far.

What your eyes can't see,

What your ears can't hear...

The good, the bad...

The love, the death...

I am, I am, I am...

Bring pure joy;

It's not too late.

Take away the wounds,

Because it's too much for one to bear...!

Stubborn Pain

Pain…
He does not go away.

Pain…
He's stubborn,
Adamant too.

Craving the spotlight,
Eager to shine bright.

Center of attention,
He makes me irrational.

Marking his presence,
Sitting on a high throne—
Guess what he says:

"Woman, I am here to stay."

Rainbow
(Beautiful Escape)

One of the rarest times

When I truly

Love me.

I feel like magic,

An alien,

A beautiful escape.

My mind becomes

A rainbow,

My heart,

The rain.

I kiss the winds,

I jump

On the hurricane.

I sync with

The earth,

Circle the fire

Like a

Tiny dot.

I don't look

For a man.

Love flows

In my veins.

My breath dances

To the rhythm

Of the music

Of my

Own beat.

Breathless

My lover makes me breathless

Not by the way he loves,

But by the way he shows me hate.

I beg, I plead,

I ask for mercy.

Then I pray for forgiveness

For the wounded heart I possess.

My eyes get heavy

From crying so hard.

My mind gets numb

From thoughts that are sad.

Worth

Why do I only write
When I feel I have no worth?

Maybe to feel a little better,
Or to boost my ego a bit more.

That I, too, exist
In a tiny world of words,
That I can also be honest
Once in a blue moon.

Maybe I only write
When I feel I am not enough
To take the judgment away
And to fill a short-term bruise.

How do I feel?

How do I feel?
If I ask myself
Trapped soul
Lost in my mind
Consumed with thoughts
Numb with the surround

Hopeful yet scared
Lonely not alone

How am I made to feel?
If I ask myself
Misunderstood all the time
Unloved and unkind
Selfish and rude

A punching tool

A human with all the faults

The loser of all sorts

Underserved to be loved

To be grateful for my beloved

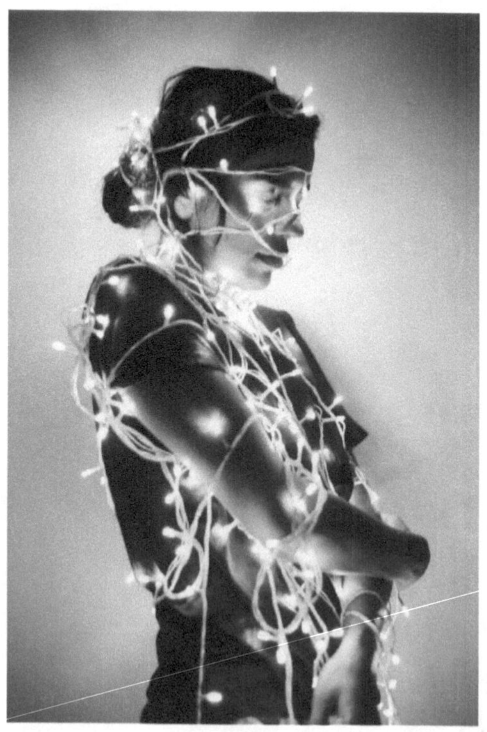

Between Sunrises and Sunsets

As I'm lying on the couch,
Sun rays splash the marble floor.

I'm watching this movie,
One I've seen countless times before.

Away from home,
In a land of young souls.
Years have passed,
Missing so many sunrises and sunsets.

Always dreamed of a better tomorrow,
Yet never felt the magic of today.
Sometimes, I overthink the sorrow—

With just a few days left to play,

Will I find joy in what's to come?

Will I finally know what it was all for?

For my biggest Fan

Do you want me to write forever?
Is this what you wish for now?

I'm okay with that.

I like writing to you,
Or about you.

It's like a salsa dance—
The words move on their own.

You said I don't write about you?
What a foolish thought.

I'd be the worst writer in this whole world
If I didn't write for my biggest fan.

Just a Crush

I don't even know him very well,
But perhaps the butterflies in my stomach can tell.
The beats of my heart whisper his name
As echoes of my thoughts dance like flame.

With just a hint of his glimpse,
My heart races a bit;
Fingers run gently through my hair,
Breaths grow deeper,
Floating everywhere.

Don't let me even start about these traitors—
The eyes.
They glare shamelessly
At him,
Desperately waiting for a look back.

That's it.

I rest my case, my friend.

I'm experiencing
The purest and sweetest kind of crush.

Same Old Story

There's no reason to talk, maybe;
We shouldn't, I guess.

It will only get messier,
As we tear each other apart,
Tempers will be lost,
Hopes will fade to dark.

Circling the same chapter,
We'll never move forward.

Shall we just battle our own demons and not regret?
Because you'll judge me for my future and also my past.

I'm tired of it—
The rights and the wrongs.

Enough of this bullshit;
Enough of this mess.

Life is nothing but a chance.
If experiences are bad,
Does that mean we should stay in our beds?
And never move an inch forward.

But we're all fighting,
Running this superficial war.

I'm the last person to ask,
What should we do right now?
Should we keep trying to talk,
Or is it time to say goodbye?

Dream Gal

Her aura is magic;

They call her an alien—

Big brown eyes,

A beautiful wide smile.

Thoughts crash like waves;

She kills softly with just a single gaze.

Holding a wild tsunami brain,

And she is the colorful rainbow after rain.

Looking through your soul—

She captivates your brain.

Warming the chill of your heart,

A ray of sunshine in a dark world.

A safe haven on earth—

Tell her

She is your ultimate dream gal.

Hurricane and Drizzle

"You're the hurricane, and I am a drizzle," he says.
"It's either coal black or milky white," he adds.

A carefully crafted lie,
Gift-wrapped for destruction, he feels.
A relic from a prior life,
A rare creation, she seems.

"Scarlet woman, lady of the night," he rates.
"Everlasting love, my one and only," he claims.

Reflection of the soul,
The echo of her sound, she feels.
Magnificent northern lights,
A sterling pound, he seems.

Sprinkle in the spring, golden monsoon; he is.

"Nothing before, nothing beyond," she whispers.

Eclipse of the Heart

I miss you too.
Is it the right time to start?

One more chance—
we'll be careful,
can we promise, just once?

Remember we never judged?
Remember—that's how it all began.

Are we really just flesh and bone?
Are you sure we've lost all hope?

Weren't we the diamond stars,
shining bright from a galaxy afar?

Light in the black night,

calm in the sounds of war.

Turn around, curious eyes,

before the total eclipse of heart.

Turn around, scientific mind—

how many times must I remind?

Without Knowing Love

I said yes to love
without knowing what love is.
My knees never felt weak,
nor did my heart race.

Why did I say yes to love,
not knowing what it meant?
Now, as I start to feel something,
I've already given my consent.

Why did I say yes to love,
without truly falling deep?

Autumn

One of those days

Some days are darker than the nights,
In the past, the light resides
One of those days,
I am not myself.
One of those days,
I need your side.

When the words gather strength,
The heart turns blind.
I write to myself,
"This is not your life."

When grips are so strong,
The roots bury deep in the soul,
You witness blood changing its color—
And all you're left with is envy.

The leaves fade to yellow,

Drought consumes the field.

One of those days,

I am not myself.

One of those days,

I lose myself.

One of those days,

I search for the light

One of those days,

I scream to feel alive.

The sad me

I feel this heaviness on my chest,
It keeps building,
Growing,
When I am alone—
Taking weight
Of my thoughts,
Of emptiness,
Of my sorrows.

I can feel it,
Sitting right there,
Waiting for me to acknowledge.
And when I do,
It keeps building,
Growing,

Taking the weight
Of my thoughts,
Of my emptiness,
Of my sorrows.

I take a breath,
Count one, two, and three,
Whisper to the shadows,
"Please let go of me.
The sad me."

Silent Tears

Sometimes you feel so sad, so deeply sad,

that you're sure your heart will burst any minute.

You seek solitude,

but you're not sure you can handle your own company.

The only way out seems to be

To brutally cut your heart into two pieces

And give one half to someone,

Who'll never return the part.

Slowly, you start hating all forms of human interaction.

Smiling humans come with an intention in your mind.

You are having trust issues.

You don't know yourself.

You genuinely don't.

You cannot go back; you cannot move forward.

Tears are resting on the edge of your eyelid,

but you keep them there only

until they burn to death.

Is there an answer?

Pointless

Teardrops command me to drop a line,

When I am SCREAMING at them to end...

This heart is much the same as an insulator,

Thousands of volts unable to create any difference...!

Fading here at every instant,

Yet labeled a home...

Thirsting to incur the diamond

By thoroughly polishing the stone...!

Everything I admire,

I am going to capture...

I reached this conclusion

When people I knew

Started turning into pictures...!

Some consider me authentic,

For some, I'm just a fuss...

I can make you believe I am an atheist,

While traveling with you in a temple bus...!

The last station is at the edge,

Where palms can kiss the faith bell...

Pointless how far these arms can stretch,

Every string is attached to this hell...!

Wounded Heart

My heart aches tonight,
But I will help myself.

This moment has come;
This moment will pass.
My heart will heal—
No external help it demands.

The wounds are deep;
They need time to mend.
I will give what they require;
I won't ask anyone
As I have in the past.

I've learned my lesson—
No more; request denied.

I learn from mistakes,
I grow from heartbreaks.

When I sought help in the past
To heal my wounded heart,
They crushed my lively soul.
They laughed behind my back.

I learn from my past;
I learn from you all.

And now I stand stubborn,
Refusing the game.

ICU

Do not cry, you.

Do not cry, me.

They'll joke about your pain,

Laugh at the tears you cry.

But you'll lose this game,

If you don't even try.

This is the moment

When 'strong' must rise.

This is the moment

Weakness stays behind.

Cry when no one's around,

Only where you know trust can be found.

Not everyone deserves your tears—

Protect your heart; that's a must.

Be your own doctor,

You know what's wrong.

Make your own medicine,

Cut out where you don't belong.

Make an appointment,

Call on your soul.

It will answer—I know.

Take it to the ICU,

The ICU within your heart.

Be your own surgeon—

Heal what's torn apart.

Operate on your broken heart

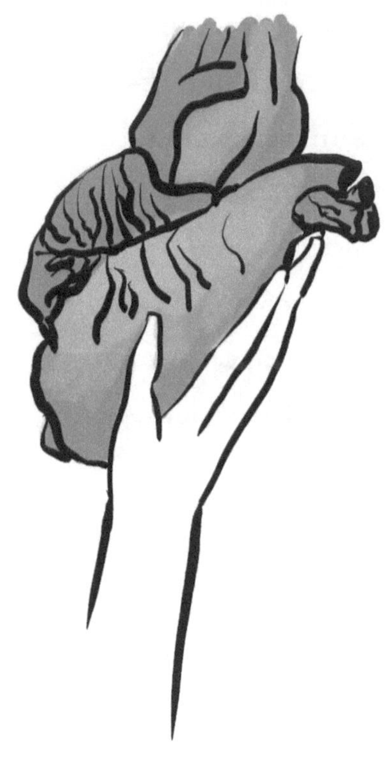

Regret

I feel it—
Regret,
Loud and clear,

Pressing hard
Against my chest.

I know you well,
I made you.

Once upon a time,
You were
A decision,
A path I chose.

Once upon a time,

you had no name.

But now,

You echo all my thoughts

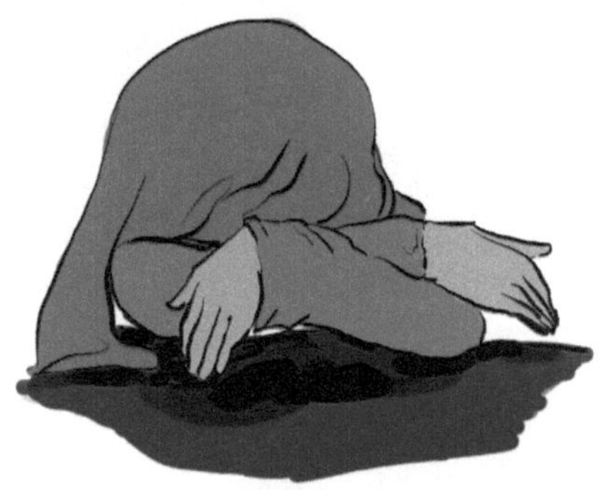

Fool's Paradise

Oh, you've killed me a thousand times
With your words and with your pride,
Slowly ripping off my skin,
Your hands cutting like a knife.

Yet I come alive like every other time,
Preparing for the next round—
You with all your weapons,
And me, facing my vulnerable side.

Like an uninvited guest in your house,
Just one room, and one more night.
Listening to your melodies,
I've wandered across many skies.

But deep down, I always knew,

This was just a fool's paradise.

He Makes Me Cry

He makes me cry more than he ever made me smile,
He thinks I'm the disease destroying his life.
He forgot how to make me laugh,
So he keeps replaying the same sad track.

Words no longer come easy to me,
Not until I feel like I'm tearing apart.
Tears keep falling on every line I write,
Their meaning fades before they can take flight.

I hope there will be a day,
When I'm not asked to change my way.
I'll be loved for who I am,
Without being ignored,
Without losing my soul.

Reconciliation

There's nothing left;
we're caught in a trap.

Our history confirms—
reconciliation
exists only in words.

Past deeds
buried so deep
are rising again from the ground.
Ghosts we thought were gone
circle us round and round.

I beg you to leave—
enough of the grief,

Enough of the fear,

enough of the scars—

they haunt,

yet never disappear.

End of all Ends

It's hard,
so damn hard
to move on

when chains are still tied
to your feet,
to your arms.

It's hard,
so damn hard
to leave someone

whom you once adored
and still love with all your heart.

The scars remain,
four walls contain
the flaws and pride
a lover can't hide.

Animals may become human;
humans were animals once.
Stars and galaxies—
too infinite to count.
Earth, a tiny dot;
you and I,
not even a speck beneath a microscope.

But why does the Universe feel so small
when heartache fills us all?
Everything fades, silent and small,
and the sun becomes just a fireball.

Your troubles expand filling all space,
as a big bang bursts within your brain.
Opposite clash;
time forgets to keep the count.

Where is the end?
The end of all this pain
when it becomes hard,
so damn hard.
Chains tied
to your feet,
to your arms.

Is there a way out?
Is there a meaning at all?
They say to leave your art,
the words and the sounds.

Reincarnated, maybe we will learn
from the mistakes of this life.

My soul replays one question:
where is the end of all ends?

Moonchild

Dark, dark days,
sun on my face.

Starry, starry nights,
blackness on my mind.

Lost, the Moonchild.

Suicidal thoughts,
trapped in a hole.
Love slapped,
punched hard,
gripped my neck,
broke both arms.

Blue became my eyes,
blue painted my life,
blue fills my days,
the blue follows my nights.

Victim blamed,
abuser celebrates.

Damage control.

Same tactics,
old are the ways.

Criminal cell,
silence groans.

No rain check—
it's a fucking storm.

The Rise of "I"

I am the ego,
I, the devil's eye.
I destroy the gods,
I make you alone.

Life keeps thrusting.
Many "I" have come,
many "I" have gone.

Historical fragile,
futuristic rise.

In my soul resides
the god of destruction,
creator topnotch.

In my spirit resides

the only

rider of my whole.

Midnight

Fooled in love and lost at heart,

A tainted soul from playing its part.

Hours pass slowly after midnight,

Yet no sleep graces thy woeful eyes

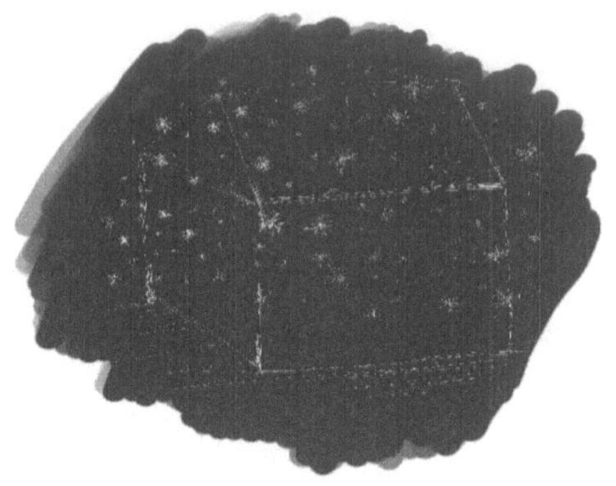

Internal Suicide

I hope you're sleeping sound.

Just so you know,
You took the peace from my mind.

I hope you're loved by those around.

Just so you know,
I talk to myself before I sleep every night.

I hope you're cherished for being redefined.

Just so you know,
I changed for myself, too, last night.

I hope you find joy in your new life.

Just so you know,
I buried a part of me last night.

Farewell of Mr. Pain

No matter what I write

How much I write

Fill all the pages

And ask for more to fill

Mr. Pain

Why you won't go

You had a home here

You loved it for long

But I don't

I don't like you, Mr Pain

I despise you, Mr Pain

You unwanted guest
Have some self-respect

Feeding on my bones and skin
Since young
Go and earn your own bread, Mr Pain

Your time is over
You cannot overstay one moment
Pack your bags
And gather all your trash, Mr Pain

Take a flight
On this stormy night
Go away far
Far away from my life, Mr Pain

Catch the next bus, you are late
My doors are locked, don't await

I will go sane from the lightening insane
You Mix with dirt during this rain, Mr Pain

Go Away

Please go far away, Mr Fucking Pain

Don't look back, Mr. Pain

Winter

Lost Traveler

Wandering through eternity,
His home stretched across open lands.

When asked where he had come from,
He simply said, "Not too far."

When asked where he planned to go,
He answered, "Somewhere afar."

As he passed them by,
A stranger asked, "Who is he?"
Whispers drifted on the breeze:
"A lost traveler," they murmured,
"Born anew, yet never at rest."

Your Society

I am not too fond of you, Society.

In fact, I despise you quietly.

Your money, your crowns, your thrones, your riots.

The fake kings you create,

The plastic queens you celebrate.

Oh yes, Society, sell bodies—why not?

Trade dreams like cheap stocks—

Empty souls, vacant eyes,

Hollow hearts, twisted with lies.

You crush the poor, left barefoot entirely,

But think you're bigger than God, don't you, Society?

Your business of love? How priceless.

Your worthless piece of power—go on, take it.

Build your palace,

Hide in closets draped in crocodile skins,

Cover your tracks with flashing sins.

Yes, keep those cameras rolling—

Everyone's watching the show, aren't they, Society?

Flash your black cards,

Oh, scream at the waiters,

Make sure you call the manager—

We all know that's the highlight of your day, Society.

Spice up your drinks,

Toss in some pills,

Stay high on your fake life,

Chasing empty thrills, Society.

Surround yourself with
People-pleasers,
Backbiters,
Selfish friends,
You, Society.

Tell everyone you're different,
Unique, open-minded,
The best of the best.
One in a million, Society.

But let me be honest—
You, me,
All of us—
We're all messed up.

Learn from Bukowski,
You, Society.

Burn this world,
Burn your souls.

Take your world out of my sight,
You, Society.

I can't bear this anymore.
I don't give a damn about your world,
Your fame,
Your status,
Your worthless wealth—
Take it to your grave,
You messed-up Society.

Bury it deep,
Take it to your grave,
You glorious, fucked-up Society.

Amateur Poem

You can call it love
or name it a fling.

There's a pleasant sadness
and sugared loneliness
I carry
wherever I go.
I am crowded
with your memories.
You say
I no longer visit your thoughts,
that I've become
just a fading trace—
a ghost slipping silently, unseen,
hiding behind a glass screen.
All my dreams

turn to verses

in an amateur poem—

and I'm left with your memories

alone.

Two Faced

The two faces of me—

One is called Left,

And the other, Right.

The two faces of me—

One is called Sunshine,

And the other, Dark Nights.

When I fell in love,

My lover married only the Left,

Craving only the Sunshine.

So I hid the Right

In the black, endless nights,

But the moon had to shine—

Ah, I was left with just Right.

It Will Pass

And I knew, even in the moment,
that it would pass.

I was sad,
so sad—
heartbroken,
helpless,
fearful,
and stressed—
so stressed.

I couldn't hold the pain.

Fingers bled
the instant I held the pen.

Pages dampened
each time I turned to the next.

I screamed at the universe—
Enough.

And I knew, even in that moment,
that it would pass.

Un-Love

Do you know the feeling
of slowly losing someone
you've known for so long?

With whom
you've shared your life—
the dreams, the fears,
the tears, the smiles.

Whose laugh was your favorite sight,
whose tears could make you cry.
Their favorite song,
a part of your playlist;
their warm hug,
your best medicine.

But it's not the same anymore.
No it's not the same anymore.

Now, you delete words,
rethink,
analyse
before you share anything.
Sometimes you don't.

You keep it all to yourself—
where it always belonged,
quietly locked within, unseen.

Do you know the feeling
when you have to un-love someone
you've loved with all you had,
to leave behind what once made you glad?
To turn them into a stranger once more—
even though you know
you never can for sure.

But they cared, and so did you.

You still do, and maybe they do too.

Yet the distance grows, silent and wide—

and perhaps they feel it, side by side.

Awakening

Are you truly living,
or just breathing through the motions?

You have all the fuel—
why is the fire still not burning?

Watching unfilled dreams
dancing in your eyes,
you're growing so nervous,
"Haven't slept in so long,
my thoughts like a restless song."

A winter's slave,
once warmed by the sun,
now relief draws near—
the long wait is finally done.

Grey Areas

Truth doesn't exist;

Love is a cruel joke,

And so are relationships.

Money changes people;

Time goes on.

There's no pure white,

nor is there black.

Grey is real,

in the middle, somewhere.

Sleepless nights,

yet we survive.

We are all on a journey—

where hate unites,

anger slides,

and violence arrives.

Guns and bombs—

the consequences

of human greed run high.

When is it enough?

Is it necessary

to work,

to have a job,

to excel at something,

to have a passion since young?

Is it necessary

to have ambitions,

to chase our dreams

and find our themes?

Is it not enough—

a roof overhead,

a meal to fill,

a few hearts to love,

and more love to give?

Is it not enough

to simply breathe in the now,

to rest in the quiet,

to let life unfold

without needing to think too much?

Small room

Will there ever be a day
when you join my night?

Or have we met again,
only never to unite?

The lighter's out of fuel,
cigarettes longing to ignite,
and damp matchsticks
don't light quite right.

How long must I wait?
Who will mark the time?
Random places,
Lost in historical fights.

I sit here in the corner,

in this small room—

lights off,

on a moonless night.

A flower vase lies on the ground,

Framed paintings scattered all around.

Some unread books, gathering dust,

Quiet on the outside, it's hard to trust.

Internal desires on a winter night,

Alone with a notepad,

I type my thoughts,

Curtains drawn tight.

Old floor,

Memories survived.

In this silence, I ponder—

Reflecting on moments

When I felt most alive?

Mirror, Mirror on the Wall

What do you truly see in the mirror?

A mask that veils the truth,

a handful of lies

parading as proof.

Shallow waters—

to dive for a quick thrill.

What do you see in the mirror?

While applying makeup,

fixing your hair,

crafting a perfect look.

What do you spot in the mirror?

A caged bird on a branch,

a wild beast,

forever trapped.

What do you see in the mirror?
Wrinkles of age
or the glow of youth?

Heavy jewels, diamonds shine,
or dust that fades with time?

Why gaze in the mirror
while hoarding your gold,
hiding it from those
who are left in the cold?

Kabira says:
"Listen, dear friend—
you live in vain,
wasting your days,
taking words while life plays."

The heart won't share the truth;

the mind keeps it concealed.

What worth is this spirit

if your life remains concealed?

Why stare into the mirror?

Love Yourself

For your own sake, love yourself.
You are beautiful—
both inside and out.
with kind eyes that shine.
You're aware most of the time.

Please, love yourself
more than anyone else can.
There's no other way—
You have to love yourself.

What if you're not perfect?
No one ever was.
You are enough—
So love yourself.

Value your differences.
Value your uniqueness.
Value this human birth.
Keep on finding your worth.

So, can you love yourself?
My dear, take a chance.
Embrace the beauty within,
and let your heart dance.

Please just love yourself.

Rise above Judgements

I was holding life—

Dry sand
clenched in my fist,
slipping through my wrist.

I held my emotions—
an ice cream cone
melting away
beneath a blazing sun.

I walked toward the end,
on a slippery road,
blindfolded.

Whispers curled around me,

telling me I'd lose,

shouts rang louder,

declaring I would fall.

The sand slipped,

my hands grew weak,

and I fell on my back.

They were right!

I fell; they laughed—

But the earth keeps spinning in its quiet dance,

The sun will rise in its golden trance,

and stars will shine in the softest night,

while the universe moves, untouched by the fight—

Endless and strong, untouched by it all,

Calm and timeless, not bothered by our fall.

Affection

Affection—
It is beautiful!

I want to talk to you,
never to hurt you,
never to be hurt by you.

No reason to speak,
no hands to hold,
no family to build,

but there are wishes for a good life
and hopes to be unforgettable.

Who are you?

I long for a love that feels so distant,
I dream of a love that shines like a star.

Longings from a past life,
filling the void—
in my mind,
my body,
and my soul.

Parched lips
yearn for a tender touch,
like a desert waits
for rain so much.
Like endless sand, waiting
for the sky to transform.

No, I don't enjoy life without you.
I hope, think, and dream of you—
from as far back as I can remember.

But tell me this—
Who are you, really?
Reveal your truth.

Gods

Once in a while,
A few thoughts cross my mind—
Some foolish questions
With no clear answer

Do I believe in the Almighty,
Or am I scared of the reverse?
Millions of gods in every way—
Which one is for me?
To whom should I pray?
Does God vary with culture, or is religion just a myth?
They say their God is different,
Then why does the definition never change?
And if true love only knows the inner beauty,
Why are countless phrases praising the outer face?
Trying to love all the way it is,

But for how long?

How long for the lies?

Isn't change the only truth

If one has to define?

If you ask me just once,

I'll sum it up in two lines—

Let's not change the gods.

Let's change the way we believe.

What is life?

A beautiful dream,

or a tragic theme?

Is life within us, or are we life?

Am I you, or are you the I?

If life is a joke,

could it be the best till date?

A clever twist,

or a quiet matrix of fate?

What lies beneath the smile?

Maybe an awkward dance

and a roll of the dice.

If you're the player,

who holds the score?

I see the crowd around,

but what's the true prize?

In this little game of ours,

what do we truly seek?

Is it joy, connection,

or just a chance to peek?

Is it love that we seek,

or peace of the mind?

But we all know one thing,

together,

we share this playground of humankind.

If Only

The thing is,
I don't want to write.

And why should I pen it down?

There is no motive to write.

If only my thoughts were weak,
and words had driven my course.

If only emotions had spoken my mind,
or maybe you had figured me out—

I wouldn't have to write.

But nothing of that sort exists.

Lonely in an overpopulated world,

birds try hard to pull the gloom apart.
The sun is appreciated only when the cold bites.

Criminals cannot stand moonlight.
Darkness masks, but never fully hides

Rehab

I'm not a fan of myself anymore,
I don't like the me I was before.
Looking for escapes,
running from reality,
taking everything for granted so casually.

Drunk and unaware
of what's in the air,
vulnerable and scared,
a weight hard to bear.

I demand rehab—
rehab for my mind,
rehab for the lines

Rehab for my doubts,

rehab to feel whole,

rehab for growing old,

rehab to soothe my soul.

Rehab for the guilt

I cannot outpace,

rehab to find myself

in a kinder place.

Breaking Free

I am leaving you first,
you selfish ones.
You took advantage of me,
then made me feel weak.

Go to hell or heaven,
whichever suits your mission.
I don't care about your fate,
nor the bitterness of your hate.

Your society?
It means nothing to me.
You do you.
The world is yours,
your life—you are free.

But please, don't block my gates.

I've survived till now,

and I'll find my own ways.